CROSSING

WRITTEN BY JEFF PRIES

Thomas Nelson
Since 1798

NASHVILLE · DALLAS MEXICO CITY RIO DE JANEIRO BEIJING

Published in Nashville, Tennessee. Thomas Nelson is a trademark of Thomas Nelson, Inc.

Published in association with the literary agency of Yates & Yates, LLP, Attorneys and Counselors, Orange, California.

Thomas Nelson, Inc. titles may be purchased in bulk for educational, business, fund-raising, or sales promotional use. For information, please e-mail SpecialMarkets@ThomasNelson.com.

Unless noted otherwise, all Scripture quotations are taken from the New Century Version®. Copyright © 2005 by Thomas Nelson, Inc. Used by permission. All rights reserved.

ISBN: 978-1-4185-3351-9

Printed in China.
08 09 10 11 12 SS 9 8 7 6 5 4 3 2 1

CONTENTS

▰▰▰ INTRODUCTION

LIQUID

Five episodes. One story.

God's Word is as true today as it was when it was written.

But for too long, we have looked at God's Word and wondered how it could possibly impact our lives. It's one thing to simply read the Bible. It's something different altogether to understand it. Far too often we read these stories about people in an ancient land, and we're left feeling flat. "What's this got to do with me?" We know in our hearts that what we're reading is true, right, and good, but we can't see any real way to apply it.

That's where *LIQUID* comes in.

LIQUID presents true-to-life stories of characters with real problems. Because what's the point in putting together a study of God's Word that doesn't deal with any of the issues we actually face? Along with each chapter in this book is a film, filled with characters that live in our world—the real world. Yet their problems and struggles mirror the same struggles found in stories in the Bible.

Jesus is the master storyteller. He helped people understand, made them contemplate, made them consider. He wasn't afraid to cut a story a couple of ways, as if he was saying, "Let me say it another way, a different way, so you can understand." He often gave answers by asking questions in return, so people would investigate, think, learn. It's how he did it, so it's why we do it. We translate ancient stories into the language of today's culture, and we ask relevant questions to help you discover the truth for yourself.

Whether you're with a small group, or simply by yourself, all we ask is that you take a deep breath, pop in the DVD, and then read through these pages and think carefully about the questions and the Scriptures. These are not questions from the SAT—they don't have definitive answers. They are designed for you to reflect upon based on your perspective. Everyone's discoveries will be different. But that's what's great about God's truth—it's one truth, but it's formed differently around each person.

It's simply about taking in, reflecting, and coming up with something useful for your life. Now at last we have an immediate, portable, relevant way to experience God's Word. A revolutionary new way to study the Bible.

LIQUID. God's Word flowing through your life.

▤▤ CROSSING

Life is a journey. All along the way we reach points where we have to decide if we're going to step out in faith and let God take our lives to a different place, or if we're going to let fear and insecurity paralyze us and keep us from crossing over. Making a crossing always calls for uncommon courage, faith, and obedience.

As God's leader, Joshua demonstrated unwavering determination in winning the land God had promised to his people, and in getting all the tribes of Israel and their families settled in the new land. In this book, we'll take a look at Joshua and the nearly two million Israelites as they cross the Jordan River to a new place—a better place, a place unimaginable based on where they stood before they crossed.

The only way to get to the other side of life's challenges and changes is to step out in faith and cross over—just as Joshua and the Israelites did. Like any crossing, it's going to take strength and courage. Are you ready?

CHAPTER 1: CHANGE

Liquid

Change. We throw the word around a lot: "I need to *change* clothes." "I think it's time to *change* jobs." We look at our lives and say, "Something has to *change*." We need a *change* of venue, or a *change* of scenery. Sometimes *change* is thrust upon us, sometimes we decide to *change* on our own. No matter how it comes about, it immediately makes things different. Sometimes exciting, sometimes fun, sometimes dreadful.

When have you had to embrace change?

Play video episode now.

Probably the most difficult time in my life was moving away when I was in junior high. New home . . . new school . . . new friends . . . I'm sorry, did I say *new* friends? I meant *no* friends. I was the new kid—sneered at, pointed at, but ultimately left alone. Change is hard, scary, and lonely. Ultimately, however, we get what we want to get out of it. We can pout, we can be angry, or we can look on the bright side and get excited about the new opportunities we've been given.

What are some things that make change difficult for the people in the film?

How does or doesn't this story represent change in people's lives today?

[1]After Moses, the servant of the LORD, died, the LORD spoke to Joshua son of Nun, Moses' assistant. [2] The LORD said, "My servant Moses is dead. Now you and all these people go across the Jordan River into the land I am giving to the Israelites. [3] I promised Moses I would give you this land, so I will give you every place you go in the land. [4] All the land from the desert in the south to Lebanon in the north will be yours. All the land from the great river, the Euphrates, in the east, to the Mediterranean Sea in the west will be yours, too, including the land of the Hittites. [5] No one will be able to defeat you all your life. Just as I was with Moses, so I will be with you. I will not leave you or forget you.

[6] "Joshua, be strong and brave! You must lead these people so they can take the land that I promised their fathers I would give them. [7] Be strong and brave. Be sure to obey all the teachings my servant Moses gave you. If you follow them exactly, you will be successful in everything you do. [8] Always remember what is written in the Book of the Teachings. Study it day and night to be sure to obey everything that is written there. If you do this, you will be wise and successful in everything. [9] Remember that I commanded you to be strong and brave. Don't be afraid, because the LORD your God will be with you everywhere you go."

¹⁰ Then Joshua gave orders to the officers of the people: ¹¹ "Go through the camp and tell the people, 'Get your supplies ready. Three days from now you will cross the Jordan River and take the land the Lord your God is giving you.' "

¹² Then Joshua said to the people of Reuben, Gad, and East Manasseh, ¹³ "Remember what Moses, the servant of the Lord, told you. He said the Lord your God would give you rest and would give you this land. ¹⁴ Now the Lord has given you this land east of the Jordan River. Your wives, children, and animals may stay here, but your fighting men must dress for war and cross the Jordan River ahead of your brothers to help them. ¹⁵ The Lord has given you a place to rest and will do the same for your brothers. But you must help them until they take the land the Lord their God is giving them. Then you may return to your own land east of the Jordan River, the land that Moses, the servant of the Lord, gave you."

¹⁶ Then the people answered Joshua, "Anything you command us to do, we will do. Any place you send us, we will go. ¹⁷ Just as we fully obeyed Moses, we will obey you. We ask only that the Lord your God be with you just as he was with Moses. ¹⁸ Whoever refuses to obey your commands or turns against you will be put to death. Just be strong and brave!"

What changes did Joshua and the people of Israel face, and what do we learn about embracing change from this passage?

CULTURAL AND HISTORICAL THOUGHTS:

The Israelites wandered in the wilderness for forty years as part of God's punishment for their lack of trust in his provision. Once that generation had died off, it was time for them to enter the Promised Land, under a new leader. Moses, their previous leader, had died and Joshua was appointed by God to succeed him (Numbers 27:18–23). Joshua had assisted Moses for many years and was well prepared for his leadership position.

Joshua's new job was to lead more than two million people into a strange new land and conquer it. This was not an act of imperialism or aggression but rather an act of judgment. Several passages in the Bible enumerate God's promises to give this land to the Israelites and the reasons for doing so. (Refer to Genesis 12:1–3; 15:16; 17:7–8; Exodus 33:1–3; Deuteronomy 4:5–8; 7:1–5; 12:2.)

Just one year earlier Moses granted the tribes of Reuben and Gad and the half-tribe of Manasseh the right to settle just east of the Promised Land. The area was excellent pastureland for their large flocks. As payback for this land grant, they were to join their fellow tribes to help conquer the Promised Land when it was time to enter it. Then, only after the land was conquered, could they return to their homes. Now it was time for them to settle this debt.

Have you ever been on a roll, feeling as though no one could beat you? I remember playing high school basketball and feeling as if I was in the zone, that I couldn't miss. I would look at the guy guarding me, and I knew I could score on him. Then their coach would bring someone different in to guard me, and I would think, *Why did they have to change it up on me? I was doing so well.* I had a similar experience as a kid playing the card game, Bridge, with my mom and grandmother. I'd have winning streaks over and over again, but then inevitably they'd tell me we had to rotate seats. I'd think, *No! Don't break the momentum. If I change right now, I'll lose my stride.* Change can mess us up. It can make things more difficult. But it can also make us stronger players.

What makes change difficult?

What are some of the benefits of change?

Look around you. I'll bet you can't turn 360 degrees without seeing someone on a cell phone. Technology has taken control of our lives— for the good or for the bad, that's up to you to decide. It's changed the way we work, the way we interact, the way we deal with people. As far as I'm concerned, I love technology. It helps me multitask, it keeps my schedule on track, it makes me much more productive. The problem is, technology is changing so fast, I can't keep up. As soon as I feel that I've figured it out, it changes on me. You see, I'm not just one model behind, I'm about three models behind. Not to mention, people have more access to me, and they've been trained to expect a quick response. The truth is, even though technology is designed to make life easier, I'm just as overwhelmed as I was five years ago.

What are ways that you see the world changing—
for the good and for the bad?

I'm getting old. Everything hurts, and I can't wait to get to bed at night. I'm slower, I'm fatter, I'm balder . . . but I'm also getting better. I'm becoming a better husband and a better father, relying more on God. We're always changing, either physically or emotionally. I guess I'm at the point where I don't run from change because I know it's an inevitable part of life. However, I do have a goal for change, no matter what the situation is, whether it's something I'm doing or something I am faced with, I challenge myself to ask, "How can I deal with it the right way? How can I change for the better?"

What changes are you facing in your life today? What makes these changes difficult? What is something exciting that may come from this change?

What are some of the most productive changes you have made in your life?
What are the things that helped you make those changes?

How can change be fun and exciting?

CHAPTER 2: RESCUE

Liquid

Have you ever dreamt of a time when you were in trouble, and as you tried to yell for help, nothing would come out of your mouth? It's one of the more frustrating dreams I've had. How often do I need help? Quite often. But how often am I willing to ask for help? That's a different story. In order for me to ask for help, I have to come to the conclusion that I can't do it on my own. Do I need help? Sure. But do I call out and ask? That's a little more difficult.

Describe a time in your life when you really needed help.

Play video episode now.

I find myself in tough spots all the time. Many times it's saying or doing something stupid, resulting in me slapping my forehead and calling myself names. Sometimes it's a potentially threatening situation. And sometimes it's even a difficult time when I just need a friend. But when I need help, who do I turn to? Who is reliable? If I'm going to actually ask for help, I sure hope that someone will be there to save me.

What are some of the things the woman in the film may have been thinking throughout this entire scenario?

[1] Joshua son of Nun secretly sent out two spies from Acacia and said to them, "Go and look at the land, particularly at the city of Jericho."

So the men went to Jericho and stayed at the house of a prostitute named Rahab.

[2] Someone told the king of Jericho, "Some men from Israel have come here tonight to spy out the land."

[3] So the king of Jericho sent this message to Rahab: "Bring out the men who came to you and entered your house. They have come to spy out our whole land."

[4] But the woman had hidden the two men. She said, "They did come here, but I didn't know where they came from. [5] In the evening, when it was time to close the city gate, they left. I don't know where they went, but if you go quickly, maybe you can catch them." [6] (The woman had taken the men up to the roof and had hidden them there under stalks of flax that she had spread out.) [7] So the king's men went out looking for the spies on the road that leads to the crossings of the Jordan River. The city gate was closed just after the king's men left the city.

[8] Before the spies went to sleep for the night, Rahab went up to the roof. [9] She said to them, "I know the LORD has given this land to your people. You frighten us very much. Everyone living in this land is terribly afraid of you [10] because we have heard how the LORD dried up the Red Sea when you came out of Egypt. We have heard how you destroyed Sihon and Og, two Amorite kings who lived east of the Jordan. [11] When we heard this, we were very frightened. Now our men are afraid to fight you because the LORD your God rules the heavens above and the earth below! [12] So now, promise me before the LORD that you will show kindness to my family just as I

showed kindness to you. Give me some proof that you will do this. ¹³ Allow my father, mother, brothers, sisters, and all of their families to live. Save us from death."

¹⁴ The men agreed and said, "It will be our lives for your lives if you don't tell anyone what we are doing. When the Lᴏʀᴅ gives us the land, we will be kind and true to you."

¹⁵ The house Rahab lived in was built on the city wall, so she used a rope to let the men down through a window. ¹⁶ She said to them, "Go into the hills so the king's men will not find you. Hide there for three days. After the king's men return, you may go on your way."

¹⁷ The men said to her, "You must do as we say. If not, we cannot be responsible for keeping this oath you have made us swear. ¹⁸ When we return to this land, you must tie this red rope in the window through which you let us down. Bring your father, mother, brothers, and all your family into your house. ¹⁹ If anyone leaves your house and is killed, it is his own fault. We cannot be responsible for him. If anyone in your house is hurt, we will be responsible. ²⁰ But if you tell anyone about this, we will be free from the oath you made us swear."

²¹ Rahab answered, "I agree to this." So she sent them away, and they left. Then she tied the red rope in the window.

²² The men left and went into the hills where they stayed for three days. The king's men looked for them all along the road, but after three days, they returned to the city without finding them. ²³ Then the two men started back. They left the hills and crossed the river and came to Joshua son of Nun and told him everything that had happened to them. ²⁴ They said, "The Lᴏʀᴅ surely has given us all of the land. All the people in that land are terribly afraid of us."

What do we learn from this passage about Rahab, the spies, and God?
What did Rahab know about God?

CULTURAL AND HISTORICAL THOUGHTS:

The Israelites were encamped at Shittim, in the "Arabah," or Jordan valley across from Jericho, ready to cross the river. As a final preparation, Joshua sent two spies to "spy the land" to determine if Jericho was heavily fortified and to find out the morale of the people.

Once in Jericho, the spies encountered danger and sought refuge at the home of Rahab, the prostitute. Jericho was surrounded by two walls that were about fifteen feet apart. Planks of wood spanned the gap, and houses were built on this foundation. Rahab's house was an ideal location, as it was one of those built right into the city wall.

Rahab knew people were looking for these spies and made a deal for her safety as well as the safety of her relatives. When Rahab asked for mercy to be shown to her family, she used the word *hesed*. *Hesed* means loyal, or faithful love based on a promise, agreement, or covenant. Sometimes the word is used in describing God's covenant love for his people, and sometimes, as is the case here, it refers to human relationships.

Soldiers from Jericho heard that there were spies in the land and came to Rahab's house, where she had hidden them. Rahab explained that the spies had already left the city. The soldiers did not search Rahab's house, since strict Eastern manners dictated that no man could enter a woman's house without her permission.

When the city of Jericho fell (Joshua 6), Rahab and her family were spared according to the promise of the spies.

I just installed a security system in my house. I'm not really sure why I installed it. I think I just wanted to feel safe. I wanted the security of my family to be in better hands than my own. After all, who doesn't want to feel safe? Who wouldn't want the people around them to feel protected? The problem is, it's set up so that every time a door opens, the alarm beeps. And I have four kids. Do you know how many times a day they open the door? It was driving us crazy, so I pulled the plug on the whole idea. I guess the protection of my family is in my hands after all. It's a frightening idea.

Where do people today look for protection or help?

How can these things sometimes let you down?

We all have that one incredible, out-of-reach, I-must-be-dreaming thing that we want. Is it a house that you admire? Do you think to yourself, *If I could have any house, it would be that one?* My friend has a great car that I love. I look at it and say, "I want that." Or maybe it's more subtle. I'll listen to someone speak, or someone tell a funny joke, in a way that only he could tell it. And I think to myself, *It would be nice to be like them, to have the ability that they have.* We do it with athletes, musicians, or people in the movies. Rahab did it. She looked out at the Israelites, and thought to herself, *I want what you have.* The great thing is, God gave it to her. He will do the same for us. Trust the provider, the protector. He'll come through.

Rahab saw God in the lives of others. What helps people see God the way Rahab did?
What keeps people from seeing God this way?

I'll never forget when I was eight years old, sitting in the back seat of my folks' car as we headed down the interstate during a southern Florida downpour. We hit something in the road, and the car spun across the freeway into oncoming traffic. Through God's protection, there was a forty-yard break in traffic. My dad restarted the car, and we pulled into the grass median. My mom was sobbing, and my brother and I just had that look of, "What just happened?!" I still look back at that day and ask "what if?" We didn't know God. I don't even think we believed in a god. But thirty-six years later, I see God in the storm, in the tragedy. I see the protector, the provider. The same protection I experienced as a kid, I need today. I just need to turn to God and ask for help. We all need protection, don't we? The question is, where is it going to come from? And what really works? The answer is God.

When have you seen the provision and protection of God in your life? Where do you need God's provision and protection in your life right now?

What is it about your walk with God that makes people say, "I want that!"?

What keeps you from seeing God as a protector and a provider?

CHAPTER 3: PROVISION

If you ask me what event in my life I will never forget, I would get in trouble if I didn't say my wedding or the birth of our first child. They were pretty memorable events. I get a little more excited when I remember my first round of golf in the '70s, or winning championships in high school. We all have these moments we will never forget. Bruce Springsteen even wrote a song about it called "Glory Days." Though I think he was mocking constant reminiscing, there's nothing wrong with it. Take a second, look back, and enjoy the experiences and events of the past. You probably have a lot of them.

What is an experience or event in your life that you will never forget?

Play video episode now.

It was his first time at bat in professional baseball, but it wasn't going so well. It had to feel lonely, different, foreign stepping up to the plate for the first time in the big leagues. The rookie began to look back, to draw inspiration from his past. It's in these moments of resistance, of pressure, of uncertainty, that drawing on our past helps. It's in these moments that it's easy to remember—to remember better days, to remember how you got to that point. In this moment, the rookie thinks of his dad and reflects on all he taught him. Then he does a great thing: he lets his dad know he never forgot him.

What were all of the things remembered or memorialized in the film?

What impact did remembering have on all the characters?

[1]Early the next morning Joshua and all the Israelites left Acacia. They traveled to the Jordan River and camped there before crossing it. [2]After three days the officers went through the camp [3]and gave orders to the people: "When you see the priests and Levites carrying the Ark of the Agreement with the LORD your God, leave where you are and follow it. [4]That way you will know which way to go since you have never been here before. But do not follow too closely. Stay about a thousand yards behind the Ark."

[5]Then Joshua told the people, "Make yourselves holy, because tomorrow the LORD will do amazing things among you."

[6]Joshua said to the priests, "Take the Ark of the Agreement and go ahead of the people." So the priests lifted the Ark and carried it ahead of the people.

[7]Then the LORD said to Joshua, "Today I will begin to make you great in the opinion of all the Israelites so the people will know I am with you just as I was with Moses. [8]Tell the priests who carry the Ark of the Agreement to go to the edge of the Jordan River and stand in the water."

⁹ Then Joshua said to the Israelites, "Come here and listen to the words of the Lᴏʀᴅ your God. ¹⁰ Here is proof that the living God is with you and that he will force out the Canaanites, Hittites, Hivites, Perizzites, Girgashites, Amorites, and Jebusites. ¹¹ The Ark of the Agreement with the Lord of the whole world will go ahead of you into the Jordan River. ¹² Now choose twelve men from among you, one from each of the twelve tribes of Israel. ¹³ The priests will carry the Ark of the Lᴏʀᴅ, the Master of the whole world, into the Jordan ahead of you. When they step into the water, it will stop. The river will stop flowing and will stand up in a heap."

¹⁴ So the people left the place where they had camped, and they followed the priests who carried the Ark of the Agreement across the Jordan River. ¹⁵ During harvest the Jordan overflows its banks. When the priests carrying the Ark came to the edge of the river and stepped into the water, ¹⁶ the water upstream stopped flowing. It stood up in a heap a great distance away at Adam, a town near Zarethan. The water flowing down to the Sea of Arabah (the Dead Sea) was completely cut off. So the people crossed the river near Jericho. ¹⁷ The priests carried the Ark of the Agreement with the Lᴏʀᴅ to the middle of the river and stood there on dry ground. They waited there while all the people of Israel walked across the Jordan River on dry land.

JOSHUA 4:1–8

[1]After all the people had finished crossing the Jordan, the Lord said to Joshua, [2] "Choose twelve men from among the people, one from each tribe. [3] Tell them to get twelve rocks from the middle of the river, from where the priests stood. Carry the rocks and put them down where you stay tonight."

[4] So Joshua chose one man from each tribe. Then he called the twelve men together [5] and said to them, "Go out into the river where the Ark of the Lord your God is. Each of you bring back one rock, one for each tribe of Israel, and carry it on your shoulder. [6] They will be a sign among you. In the future your children will ask you, 'What do these rocks mean?' [7] Tell them the water stopped flowing in the Jordan when the Ark of the Agreement with the Lord crossed the river. These rocks will always remind the Israelites of this."

[8] So the Israelites obeyed Joshua and carried twelve rocks from the middle of the Jordan River, one rock for each of the twelve tribes of Israel, just as the Lord had commanded Joshua. They carried the rocks with them and put them down where they made their camp.

What lessons about defining moments do you learn from this passage?
What do you learn about God from this passage?

CULTURAL AND HISTORICAL THOUGHTS:

Joshua and the people crossed the Jordan in the spring, when the river was overflowing its banks. God instructed Joshua to send the priests carrying the ark of the covenant into the river first, and, once the river stopped flowing, had them continue on dry ground to the middle of the riverbed. The people would then cross over on dry ground. The Israelites would have heard the stories of how their ancestors crossed over the Red Sea with Moses many years before (Exodus 14) and would be excited to see God's power do the same for them now.

The people were instructed to keep their distance (at least a half mile) from the ark, as it was Israel's most sacred treasure and a symbol of God's presence and power. The priests kept their position in the middle of the riverbed until each of the more than two million Israelites crossed over the dry riverbed. Then they waited there while a representative from each of the twelve tribes came back to the middle of the river and gathered one stone each to create a memorial for this miraculous event. This memorial would be a constant reminder for the Israelites that made the trip, for their children, and for future generations. They would remember God's power and provision in their lives.

"Never Forget." Every now and then you will see these bumper stickers, and they take you back to a life-defining moment. A moment when you realized that one way or another, American life would never be the same. We became vulnerable, fair game. "Never Forget." I probably don't even need to remind you of what the sticker is talking about: September 11, 2001. "Never forget." For some reason, I don't think we ever will.

What are some life-defining moments that you or someone you know has experienced?

There is this craze around town. Parties are thrown, invitations are sent, houses are packed out. People wait in anticipation all week for it. When the weekend finally rolls around, what are they doing? Creating photo albums. The idea that a photo album party is the talk of the town is interesting to me, almost comical. But people love them. I ask them what is the most fun part of the party? They all say the same thing: looking back at old pictures and laughing, telling stories, and reliving the moments. People are building monuments of their old memories. They are not only enjoying the beauty of looking back, but they're also making sure they never forget.

What monuments or memorials do you have in your life to remind you of God's blessing in your life?

I have to admit that I'm not very good at celebrating things. No, I'm worse than that . . . I stink at celebrating. Probably because I'm always moving on to the next thing, so I forget to celebrate the past. Why? Because I have a whole future ahead. I don't naturally dwell on history.

I was the first person inducted into the Baseball Hall of Fame at my high school. The first words out of my mouth were thank you. But I wasn't saying thank you for voting me in. I was saying thank you for helping me celebrate something I wouldn't naturally celebrate myself. But looking back is important. Celebrating is critical. The old me would have taken the trophy they gave me and put it in a box in my garage, but I didn't. I put it on a shelf in the den, kind of tucked in a cubby. No one can really see it but me, but at least I know it's there. It's a memory . . . a great memory that I shouldn't forget.

How do we often memorialize or build monuments to things in our lives?

What could you to do to celebrate the things God has done in your life? Describe what that might look like.

We can be forgetful people. What are the reasons you tend to forget what God has done for you?

What are some things that help us to remember?

CHAPTER 4: BARRIERS

Liquid

Have you ever conquered something impressive . . . no, not just impressive, but seemingly insurmountable? The kind of task where you admit to yourself afterwards, "I wasn't sure if I could do that or not." We have all had those conquering moments, the kind that give us a real sense of accomplishment. But notice the word *conquered*. To conquer something suggests being up against huge odds, or battling a strong enemy. You didn't just do something; you conquered it. And when you finished, somewhere deep down you threw up your arms and yelled, "Yes!"

What is something in your life that you've conquered with some degree of satisfaction?

Play video episode now.

I kept wanting to know why the guy in the film didn't just stand up. The entire time I'm waiting for him to surf. I've tried surfing a couple of times, and it's not as easy as it looks. So when I watched the film, I thought the guy's obstacle had to be just getting on his feet. But not this guy. He had bigger obstacles. I love his smile, his attitude. Having the right frame of mind is one of the biggest parts of tackling any challenge. Even though he knew he would never be getting on his feet, he kept the right perspective. The obstacle for me in surfing is standing up. The obstacle for this guy . . . well, you tell me.

What are all the obstacles the surfer faced—both seen and unseen?

What were the things that helped the surfer overcome his obstacles?

¹³ Joshua was near Jericho when he looked up and saw a man standing in front of him with a sword in his hand. Joshua went to him and asked, "Are you a friend or an enemy?"

¹⁴ The man answered, "I am neither. I have come as the commander of the LORD's army."

Then Joshua bowed facedown on the ground and asked, "Does my master have a command for me, his servant?"

¹⁵ The commander of the LORD's army answered, "Take off your sandals, because the place where you are standing is holy." So Joshua did.

JOSHUA 6:1–27

¹ The people of Jericho were afraid because the Israelites were near. They closed the city gates and guarded them. No one went into the city, and no one came out.

² Then the LORD said to Joshua, "Look, I have given you Jericho, its king, and all its fighting men. ³ March around the city with your army once a day for six days. ⁴ Have seven priests carry trumpets made from horns of male sheep and have them march in front of the Ark. On the seventh day march around the city seven times and have the priests blow the trumpets as they march. ⁵ They will make one long blast on the trumpets. When you hear that sound, have all the people give a loud shout. Then the walls of the city will fall so the people can go straight into the city."

⁶ So Joshua son of Nun called the priests together and said to them, "Carry the Ark of the Agreement. Tell seven priests to carry trumpets and march in front of it." ⁷ Then Joshua ordered the people, "Now go! March around the city. The soldiers with weapons should march in front of the Ark of the Agreement with the LORD."

[8] When Joshua finished speaking to the people, the seven priests began marching before the LORD. They carried the seven trumpets and blew them as they marched. The priests carrying the Ark of the Agreement with the LORD followed them. [9] Soldiers with weapons marched in front of the priests, and armed men walked behind the Ark. The priests were blowing their trumpets. [10] But Joshua had told the people not to give a war cry. He said, "Don't shout. Don't say a word until the day I tell you. Then shout." [11] So Joshua had the Ark of the LORD carried around the city one time. Then they went back to camp for the night.

[12] Early the next morning Joshua got up, and the priests carried the Ark of the LORD again. [13] The seven priests carried the seven trumpets and marched in front of the Ark of the LORD, blowing their trumpets. Soldiers with weapons marched in front of them, and other soldiers walked behind the Ark of the LORD. All this time the priests were blowing their trumpets. [14] So on the second day they marched around the city one time and then went back to camp. They did this every day for six days.

[15] On the seventh day they got up at dawn and marched around the city, just as they had on the days before. But on that day they marched around the city seven times. [16] The seventh time around the priests blew their trumpets. Then Joshua gave the command: "Now, shout! The LORD has given you this city! [17] The city and everything in it are to be destroyed as an offering to the LORD. Only Rahab the prostitute and everyone in her house should remain alive. They must not be killed, because Rahab hid the two spies we sent out. [18] Don't take any of the things that are to be destroyed as an offering to the LORD. If you take them and bring them into our camp, you yourselves will be destroyed, and you will bring trouble to all of Israel. [19] All the silver and gold and things made from bronze and iron belong to the LORD and must be saved for him."

[20] When the priests blew the trumpets, the people shouted. At the sound of the trumpets and the people's shout, the walls fell, and everyone ran straight into the city. So the Israelites defeated that city. [21] They completely destroyed with the sword every living thing in the city—men and women, young and old, cattle, sheep, and donkeys.

²² Joshua said to the two men who had spied out the land, "Go into the prostitute's house. Bring her out and bring out those who are with her, because of the promise you made to her." ²³ So the two men went into the house and brought out Rahab, her father, mother, brothers, and all those with her. They put all of her family in a safe place outside the camp of Israel.

²⁴ Then Israel burned the whole city and everything in it, but they did not burn the things made from silver, gold, bronze, and iron. These were saved for the Lord. ²⁵ Joshua saved Rahab the prostitute, her family, and all who were with her, because Rahab had helped the men he had sent to spy out Jericho. Rahab still lives among the Israelites today.

²⁶ Then Joshua made this oath:
"Anyone who tries to rebuild this city of Jericho
    will be cursed by the Lord.
The one who lays the foundation of this city
    will lose his oldest son,
and the one who sets up the gates
    will lose his youngest son."
²⁷ So the Lord was with Joshua, and Joshua became famous through all the land.

What was God's plan for conquering Jericho? Why did Joshua believe God's plan would work?

CULTURAL AND HISTORICAL THOUGHTS:

After crossing the Jordan River, the Israelites began to conquer Canaan, starting with the city of Jericho. Jericho was one of the oldest cities in the world. In some places it had fortified walls up to twenty-five feet high and twenty feet thick. Soldiers were stationed on top of the walls and could see for miles. Jericho was a symbol of military power and strength and was considered "invincible" to the Canaanites.

God's plan to destroy the city of Jericho was designed to accomplish several things. First, by placing priests carrying the ark out front instead of a massive military stance, it showed that this victory was God's. Secondly, the presence of the fighting men surrounding the city for six days in a row would accentuate the terror felt in the city. Thirdly, the unconventional military strategy was a test of the Israelites' faith and their willingness to follow God with no questions asked. The blowing of the horns has a special significance. They had been instructed to blow the same horns used in the religious festivals in their battles to remind them that their victory would come from the Lord, not their own military might (Numbers 10:9).

Obstacles are everywhere. They cause me to lie awake at night, worrying about how I'm going to deal with the situation. They keep me from my sleep, which I do not appreciate. Sometimes it's a relational obstacle, or an issue at work. Other times it's financial problems, or family issues. They all leave me wondering, *How am I going to deal with this? Can I even deal with this? Where do I start?* For me, the most frightening obstacles are the ones I don't know how to tackle. The ones that are hazy, with no clear way around. But there are ways . . . there are always ways.

What walls and obstacles do people today deal with in their lives, and what do they do to try to knock those walls down?

Think about life: if you didn't have obstacles, what would happen? I know for me, my pride would puff me up like a blowfish. I would rely on myself, feeling as if I could handle anything. I would convince myself that I didn't need others, I didn't need God. Though obstacles may seem bad at the time, they have their advantages. When we are faced with the "against all odds" moments in life, we have a tendency to rise to the occasion, or at least try. Many times, though, the only way through is by relying on God's help. More than anything else, obstacles have that great ability to draw us to God.

What walls in your life need to come down?

What steps are you prepared to take to let God break them down?

I am a public speaker. No one would know it, but it terrifies me to get up in front of people, almost to the point of being ill before I step onstage. This is one of my biggest obstacles—one that I face on a weekly basis. I also have relational obstacles. I wish I could be more open with people. I worry about paying the bills, wonder how I'm going to pay for all four of my kids to go to college. I could go on . . . and on . . . and on . . . . I have plenty of obstacles. But the true question is, "How do I overcome them?"

Based on what Joshua 5:13–15 and 6:1–27 tells us, what should be our strategy for dealing with barriers or obstacles in our life? What should our expectation be?

What are obstacles in your life that you have overcome?
What helped you overcome them?

What are some obstacles that you have seen other people overcome?

CHAPTER 5: CONSEQUENCES

We all have memories of doing something wrong as children. We would sneak something we weren't supposed to have, call someone a name we weren't supposed to say, watch a TV show we weren't supposed to watch. When we didn't get caught, we began thinking, *This is easy! No one has to know.* We felt invincible. After all, what's the worst that could happen?

We were young, and we didn't know what we've learned since then: if you do something wrong, someday you'll get caught.

Tell about a time as a kid when you did something wrong and didn't get caught.

Play video episode now.

Who wouldn't want to stumble across a box of gold? Don't you daydream about that—instant wealth? It's not easy to find a box full of gold. You know what's even harder? Finding gold and not keeping it. It's easy to believe the decision would be black-and-white, that we would do the right thing in that situation. But come on, the thought of doing what the guy in the film did wouldn't cross your mind? The truth is that no matter what you stumble upon, it's never enough. It's what makes a guy with a bag full of gold stretch for a buck . . . and die.

How would the story have been different if the guys had told the owner of the house about the gold?

[1] But the Israelites did not obey the LORD. There was a man from the tribe of Judah named Achan. (He was the son of Carmi and grandson of Zabdi, who was the son of Zerah.) Because Achan kept some of the things that were to be given to the LORD, the LORD became very angry at the Israelites.

[2] Joshua sent some men from Jericho to Ai, which was near Beth Aven, east of Bethel. He told them, "Go to Ai and spy out the area." So the men went to spy on Ai.

[3] Later they came back to Joshua and said, "There are only a few people in Ai, so we will not need all our people to defeat them. Send only two or three thousand men to fight. There is no need to send all of our people." [4] So about three thousand men went up to Ai, but the people of Ai beat them badly. [5] The people of Ai killed about thirty-six Israelites and then chased the rest from the city gate all the way down to the canyon, killing them as they went down the hill. When the Israelites saw this, they lost their courage.

[6] Then Joshua tore his clothes in sorrow. He bowed facedown on the ground before the Ark of the LORD and stayed there until evening. The leaders of Israel did the same thing. They also

threw dirt on their heads to show their sorrow. [7] Then Joshua said, "Lord GOD, you brought our people across the Jordan River. Why did you bring us this far and then let the Amorites destroy us? We would have been happy to stay on the other side of the Jordan. [8] Lord, there is nothing I can say now. Israel has been beaten by the enemy. [9] The Canaanites and all the other people in this country will hear about this and will surround and kill us all! Then what will you do for your own great name?"

[10] The LORD said to Joshua, "Stand up! Why are you down on your face? [11] The Israelites have sinned; they have broken the agreement I commanded them to obey. They took some of the things I commanded them to destroy. They have stolen and lied and have taken those things for themselves. [12] That is why the Israelites cannot face their enemies. They turn away from the fight and run, because I have commanded that they be destroyed. I will not help you anymore unless you destroy everything as I commanded you.

[13] "Now go! Make the people holy. Tell them, 'Set yourselves apart to the LORD for tomorrow. The LORD, the God of Israel, says some of you are keeping things he commanded you to destroy. You will never defeat your enemies until you throw away those things.

[14] Tomorrow morning you must be present with your tribes. The Lord will choose one tribe to stand alone before him. Then the Lord will choose one family group from that tribe to stand before him. Then the Lord will choose one family from that family group to stand before him, person by person. [15] The one who is keeping what should have been destroyed will himself be destroyed by fire. Everything he owns will be destroyed with him. He has broken the agreement with the Lord and has done a disgraceful thing among the people of Israel!'"

[16] Early the next morning Joshua led all of Israel to present themselves in their tribes, and the Lord chose the tribe of Judah. [17] So the family groups of Judah presented themselves, and the Lord then chose the family group of Zerah. When all the families of Zerah presented themselves, the family of Zabdi was chosen. [18] And Joshua told all the men in that family to present themselves. The Lord chose Achan son of Carmi. (Carmi was the son of Zabdi, who was the son of Zerah.)

¹⁹ Then Joshua said to Achan, "My son, tell the truth. Confess to the LORD, the God of Israel. Tell me what you did, and don't try to hide anything from me." ²⁰ Achan answered, "It is true! I have sinned against the LORD, the God of Israel. This is what I did: ²¹ Among the things I saw was a beautiful coat from Babylonia and about five pounds of silver and more than one and one-fourth pounds of gold. I wanted these things very much for myself, so I took them. You will find them buried in the ground under my tent, with the silver underneath."

²² So Joshua sent men who ran to the tent and found the things hidden there, with the silver. ²³ The men brought them out of the tent, took them to Joshua and all the Israelites, and spread them out on the ground before the LORD. ²⁴ Then Joshua and all the people led Achan son of Zerah to the Valley of Trouble. They also took the silver, the coat, the gold, Achan's sons, daughters, cattle, donkeys, sheep, tent, and everything he owned. ²⁵ Joshua said, "I don't know why you caused so much trouble for us, but now the LORD will bring trouble to you." Then all the people threw stones at Achan and his family until they died. Then the people burned them. ²⁶ They piled rocks over Achan's body, and they are still there today. That is why it is called the Valley of Trouble. After this the LORD was no longer angry.

What was Achan's sin, and what were the repercussions of his sin?

God's deliverance of the Israelites in their battles was dependant on their faithfulness and obedience. Since they had breached that obedience, God did not deliver victory into the hands of the Israelites in the battle at Ai. Instead thirty-six men lost their lives, and the Israelites lost their confidence. The men tore their clothing and threw dust on their heads as signs of deep mourning before God. They went before God in deep humility and sorrow to receive his instructions.

In preparation to approach God to deal with the sin that was present in the nation of Israel, the Israelites had to undergo purification rites like those performed in preparation for crossing the Jordan River (Joshua 3:5). Once their hearts were "pure," they could once again approach God. In a dramatic search that went from tribe to tribe, then family to family, it was discovered that Achan had hoarded some of the booty for himself—a complete act of defiance with consequences that affected the entire nation of Israel, as it was a national law and therefore a national disobedience. Achan's entire family was stoned and burned so that no trace of the sin would remain in Israel. A memorial was built where Achan and his family were stoned and burned and will forever be called the Valley of Trouble.

Sin is everywhere. You don't even have to look to find it; the junk in the world is right in front of your face. What bugs me is that no one looks closely enough at the junk to see what happens when you grab it. We want to act as if nothing happens, as though it doesn't matter. But ask the guy who had an affair and then gets to see his kids every other Christmas if it matters. Ask the girl who lost her job because she was caught stealing if it matters. They would probably say, "Why didn't anybody tell me?" It matters.

What are some of the ramifications of sin we see in the world today?

We've all made our mistakes. I have my share of them—some bigger than others, some more secretive. I don't want to talk about my sin to anyone. Who does? But if I were really healthy, if I really wanted to avoid making similar mistakes in the future, I would tell someone—a friend, a family member, someone close to me—just to keep me accountable. If I were smart, I would tell God, too, because he already knows. And he's really the only one who can keep me from stumbling again.

Describe a time in your life when you went down the wrong road. How did that choice impact your life?

What issue(s) of sin are you struggling with in your life right now? What do you fear the ramifications of your sin could be?

Sin and death are tough topics. That's part of the reason why I used to dislike going to church, because it's the church that always wants to talk about them. I would think, *Why does the church keep bringing this up? Let it go! It's uncomfortable.* But that's exactly why we need to talk about sin and death—because we need to know how to deal with these issues. The big mistake is not only biting on the temptations of life. The big mistake is thinking they won't hurt us. Open up . . . if not to others, at least to God.

How do people try to justify their sin?

How much does God play into your decision making?

What is an area in your life that you are struggling with right now?
What might the ramifications be of going down that road?

What makes taking the "gold" so enticing?

What do you get out of going down the wrong path?

What feelings do you get when you make the right choice?

When you mess up, who in your life does it affect, and how?

LEADER'S GUIDE

■ NOTE TO LEADERS

As leaders, we have tried to make this experience as easy for you as possible. Don't try to do too much during your time together as a group—just ask and listen, and direct when necessary.

The questions have a flow, a progression, and are designed to get people talking. If you help the group start talking early on, they will continue to talk. You will notice that the questions start out easy and casual, creating a theme. The theme continues throughout the session, flowing through casual topics, then into world affairs, and then they begin getting personal.

When the questions ask about the Bible, spend time there. Dig in and scour the passage. Keep looking. You and your group will discover that looking into the Bible can be fun and interesting. Maybe you already know that, but there will be people in your group who don't—people who are afraid of their Bibles, or who don't think they can really study them.

Remember, we are seeking life change. This will happen by taking God's Word and applying it to your life, and to the lives of the people you are with. That's the goal for each person in the group. Fight for it.

■■■ TIPS

So, are you a little nervous? Guess what—I get scared too. I always have a little apprehension when it comes to leading a group. It's what keeps me on my toes! Here are some things to keep in mind as you're preparing.

Think about your group. How does this week's topic relate to your group? Is this going to be an easy session? Is this going to be a challenge? The more at ease you are with the topic, the better the experience will be for your group.

Go over the leader's material early, and try to get to know the questions. Sometimes there are multiple questions provided at the end of the chapters. These are extra questions that can be used as supplemental questions at any point throughout the discussion. Look over these extra questions and see if any of them jump out at you. Don't feel that you have to address each question, but they are there if you need them. My worst nightmare is to be leading a group and, with thirty minutes still left on the clock, we run out of questions and there's nothing left to talk about . . . so we sit there and stare at one another in painful silence.

Just remember to keep moving through all the questions. The most important goal of this study is to get personal and see how to apply biblical truths to your own life. When you're talking about how a passage plays out in the world today, a common mistake is to not take it deep enough . . . not to push the envelope and move it from what "they" should do to what "I" should do. As a leader, you will struggle with how much to push, how deep to dig. Sometimes it will be just right; sometimes you will push too hard, or sometimes not hard enough. Though it can be nerve-racking, it's the essence of being a leader.

Here are a few more tips:

- Get them talking, laughing, and having fun.
- Don't squelch emotion. Though it may tend to make you uncomfortable, to the point where you'll want to step in and rescue the moment, remember that leaders shouldn't always interfere.
- Jump in when needed. If the question is tough, make sure to model the answer. Try to be open about your own life. Often, the group will only go as deep as you are willing to go.
- When you look in the Bible for answers, don't quit too soon. Let people really search.
- Don't be afraid of quiet.
- Lead the group—don't dominate it.

These are just a few things to think about before you begin.

▉▉▉ CHAPTER 1: CHANGE

> **When have you had to embrace change?**

This week's film vignette addresses one of life's most stressful changes—moving. While change in and of itself is neither good nor bad, it can often be difficult.

Keep the first question fun and light. Most people will feel comfortable answering it, because it draws on their life experience. Try to model a change in your life that is not painful and hard, so people don't take it down the wrong road. Make sure you don't spend too much time with this question. It could lend itself to a lot of discussion, but there's much more to come.

What are some things that make change difficult for the people in the film?

Some of the difficulties are:

- For the girl: reflecting on the past, great memories, lifelong moments in the house, leaving a boyfriend, going to a new place with a new school, facing the unknown.
- For the mom: seeing the pain on her daughter's face, having to move without the father, the physical toll of loading up the family and taking them to a different place.

How does and/or doesn't this story represent change in people's lives?

Change is hard, change can be fun and exciting, it can lead to a better place right away; but change doesn't always immediately take the shape of a beautiful new house, and it doesn't always put a smile on your face.

What changes did Joshua and the people of Israel face, and what do we learn about embracing change from this passage?

Tip: Remember that the goal of the question is to see what is in the passage. Encourage the group to look for all the facts related to the changes that Joshua and the people of Israel faced.

CHALLENGES OF CHANGE

- Change of leadership (Joshua 1:1–2): Moses had died, and Joshua was given the task of leading the people into the Promised Land; it was a new job for Joshua and a new leader for the people.
- Change of location (vv. 3–4): the people had been wandering in the desert for forty years; they were going from temporary housing to permanent residence.
- Stress of moving (v. 11): they only had three days to pack.
- From being in motion to being at rest (v. 13): they could now settle down and find rest.
- Temporary separation from family (v. 14): wives, children, and cattle stayed put while the men went to conquer their new territory.

KEYS TO EMBRACING CHANGE

- Remember, God is with you and he won't fail or abandon you (Joshua 1:5).
- Strength and courage are essential to embracing change (vv. 6–7, 9, 18).
- God's Word is key: read it, meditate on it, obey it (v. 8).
- Don't forget the past (vv. 13, 17), but also don't get stuck in it.
- Follow the leader(s) God provides to help you get through the change (vv. 16–17).

What makes change difficult in people's lives?
What might some of the benefits of change be for people?

Changes are frequently unexpected. They disrupt our sense of order, unhinge our plans, and frustrate our hopes. Change pushes us beyond our comfort zone. Without change, however, we tend to drift into the undisturbed life. God uses the challenges of change to strengthen our character and draw us closer to him.

Tip: Often, answers will tend to go down one direction. In this case, people may tend to see change as bad, or people may tend to see change as good. As a leader, make sure they explore both facets of change.

What changes are you facing in your life today? What makes them difficult? What makes them hard? What is something exciting that may come from these changes?

Don't you sometimes just wish that life would stand still? Who among us doesn't have a hard time with change? We feel safe with the familiar, comfortable with those things we are used to. But there is only one constant throughout our lives—change.

Every person in your group is likely facing change of one kind or another. The blessing of change is that the God who never changes is always near to cause all things to work together for good. Remember, everyone is experiencing change in one way or another. Don't let people off the hook when they say they aren't experiencing change. Also remember that change can be embarrassing, so don't come on too strong with people.

▬ CHAPTER 2: RESCUE

Describe a time in your life when you really needed help.

Life's adventures sometimes leave us feeling as though we need to Instant Message God, saying, "Help! Now!" Begin by sharing a life experience that left you feeling desperate and in need of help. Be sure to tell what God's provision was for your time of need. This could go a lot of ways. At this point in the group discussion, look to the lighter side. Maybe tell a story of when you were working on the roof and the ladder fell over and you got stuck on the roof. Try to avoid the more emotional stories. Save that for later in the study.

> **What are some of the things the woman in the film may have been thinking throughout this entire scenario?**

There's nothing worse than being all alone late at night, stranded. The woman must have had a whole lot running through her head: *What am I doing here? No one will help me. My stupidity put me in this situation. This could turn out really badly. Thank goodness for the tow-truck driver.*

Rahab was a harlot (Joshua 2:1) whose house was watched and well known by all the king's men (vv. 2–3); she was willing to lie to the king's men, risking her own life, to save two foreign spies (v. 4); she hid the spies on her roof under piles of dried flax and sent the king's men on a wild goose chase (vv. 4–7); she believed that Israel would conquer Jericho and that God would give them the land (v. 9); she knew and trusted the God of Israel based on her limited knowledge of his mighty acts (he dried up the Red Sea so the people could cross over, and he destroyed two Amorite kings, Sihon and Og (vv. 10–11); she was not only concerned about her own safety, but that of her immediate and extended family (vv. 12–13); she knew she needed help and wasn't ashamed to ask for it (vv. 12–13); her house was on the city wall, offering an easy escape route to the spies (v. 15); she helped the spies escape (vv. 15, 22–24); God had plans for Rahab that no one could see at the time.

The spies were secretly sent to check out Jericho (Joshua 2:1); the spies were observed by the king of Jericho, who questioned Rahab about them (vv. 2–3); when Rahab asked for protection, the spies believed they could provide it (vv. 14, 17–20); the spies accomplished their mission and reported back to Joshua that God would give them all of the land he had promised them (v. 24).

God uses people we wouldn't necessarily choose (Joshua 2:1); he reveals himself to people who have open hearts toward him (vv. 9–11); God provides for and protects people who trust him (vv. 15–16, 23–24); God is always faithful to prepare the way for his people (v. 24).

What does Rahab know about God?

She knows that God does what he says he will do (keeps his promises) and that he protects and saves his people.

Where do people today look for protection or help? How can these things sometimes let you down?

They look to their abilities, power, wealth, influence, investments, the government, friends, and family. All of our temporal and tangible sources of protection or help can be erased in the blink of an eye. We've seen this throughout history as people lose everything in the face of a natural disaster. Of course, when faced with nothing, people also begin realizing that they need God.

Help and protection sometimes come from the least-expected sources or people. We should not be surprised by God's methods of intervention in our lives.

When have you seen the provision and protection of God in your life?
Where do you need God's provision and protection in your life right now?

Remind the group of what Rahab knew: God keeps his promises and protects and saves his people. Ask group members to share life stories of God keeping his promises, protecting, and saving them in their lives. These are **two** big questions. Don't let one get lost in the other. Seeing how God provided in the past will help in seeing that he will provide today. Be vulnerable so others will be.

▬▬ CHAPTER 3: PROVISION

> What is an experience or event in your life that you will never forget?

Our lives are filled with important experiences and events. Here are just a few your group members might mention: high school or college graduation, a first date, getting married, the birth of a child, a death in the family, a career or job change, a family trip, an illness or accident. Do your best to keep it positive, fun, and light.

> What were all of the things remembered or memorialized in the film? What impact did remembering have on all the characters?

Possible answers: Hitting tips from dad, the flagpole, the idea that he can do it, the ball sent to the father, the father remembering what he said to the son.

What lessons about defining moments and God do you learn from this passage?

INSIGHTS

- God is holy, and we are not to approach him irreverently or disrespectfully (Joshua 3:4).
- God spiritually prepares us for defining moments (v. 5).
- He always goes before us and makes his presence and power evident (v. 6).
- He wants us to understand that he is a miracle-working God (vv. 10–13).
- We'll only experience his might and power if we are willing to step out in faith in spite of the "raging waters" we see ahead (v. 14).
- He challenges us to trust him, to believe that he'll come through at the high-risk moments of life.
- God wants us to be continually reminded of the times in our lives when he has been there with us. Establishing memorials helps us remember the special events and moments in times (Joshua 4:5–7).

What are some life-defining moments that you or someone you know has experienced?

Defining moments can look different for different people, obviously. Some people may say a moment when they became popular, accumulated wealth, were recognized for achievements, won something, or were accepted in the right social circles. For others, life may have thrown them a curve ball and they're faced with rebellious or drug-addicted children, bankruptcy, health problems, marital disintegration, or job loss, and these have become their self-defining moments. For others, a birth of a child, becoming a Christian, or getting married. The point? The answers could be anything. Don't make one right or one wrong; they are what they are—defining moments.

What monuments or memorials do you have to remind you of God's presence and power in your life?

In Scripture, *memorial* comes from a word that means "to prick, to pierce, or to penetrate the memory." Remember the rainbow? The tablets of stone inscribed with the Ten Commandments? The Passover, the Lord's Supper, the Cross? These all remind us that God has been at work in our lives.

Encourage group members to think about the places in their lives where God has been active. Was it when they first came to know Christ? When they were baptized? When God healed them from a serious illness? When he delivered them from an addiction? When a family member came to know Christ?

How can we create a memorial when God has done a work in our lives? By writing it down, sharing with others what God has done for us, and by using the past as a foundation for the future.

People are great at remembering the moment, but creating a memorial to the moment is a different story. Have them focus on not just the moment, but the memorial.

CHAPTER 4: BARRIERS

> What is something in your life that you have conquered with some degree of satisfaction?

Everyone has faced an obstacle. Make sure you open up and share with the group. The direction you point your answer will be the direction the group will point theirs. If you share a heavy situation with them, they will model their answers after yours. Try to keep the first question light and fun, if possible.

> What are all the obstacles the surfer faced—both seen and unseen? What were the things that helped the surfer overcome his obstacles?

The obvious obstacle was the surfer's paralysis. He also probably faced obstacles of attitude, mind-set, and accepting challenges. What helped him? Being able to reflect back into the past; being supported by friends; an enjoyment of being in the water. He surfed the best way available to him. He enjoyed lying on the board, because that was all he could do, and he was going to make the best of it. He celebrated success at the end.

What was God's plan for conquering Jericho? Why did Joshua believe God's plan would work?

God sent the commander of the Lord's army to deliver the battle plan to Joshua. Joshua recognized the man as an angel of superior rank and fell with his face to the ground in reverence (Joshua 5:14).

Battle Plan for taking Jericho: The entire army was to march around the city once a day for six days (Joshua 6:3). Seven priests were to walk ahead of the ark, each one carrying a ram's horn (6:4). On the seventh day the army was to march around the city seven times with the priests blowing the horns. Then when the priests gave one long blast on the horns, all of the people were to shout as loud as they could, and the walls would collapse (6:5). God's instructions did not involve any trenches to be dug, no battering rams to be drawn up, nor any military preparations made. God was commanding the army, and Joshua and the people trusted his plan.

What walls and obstacles do people today deal with in their lives, and what do they do to try to knock those walls down?

Sometimes the obstacle we face involves our personal finances. Or it might involve someone at work who is holding us back or with whom we have a personality conflict. Other obstacles people face are irreversible health issues, insurmountable family problems, anger, resentment, and fear. People frequently take things into their own hands or focus too much time and energy on the obstacle itself. Sometimes we choose to ignore the walls, hoping they just disappear or become somebody else's obstacle.

Remember that this question is designed to help people make a connection between the "way it was" then and the "way it is" now. Group members' responses should be generalizations, not personalized at this point.

What walls in your life need to come down? What steps are you prepared to take to let God break them down?

We all have walls in our lives that seem impossibly permanent. And the truth is, they won't come down unless we are willing to follow God's plan. Walls like bitterness, anger, and resentment stand stubbornly rooted in our lives. Not unless we follow God's Word and tell him we're ready to trust him to bring them down for good, will we experience a "Jericho" ending to these walls.

Tip: People want to talk about these things. Be vulnerable in your life, so they will be vulnerable in theirs. The best way for these walls to start coming down is for people to start talking about them.

CHAPTER 5: CONSEQUENCES

Tell about a time as a kid when you did something "bad" and didn't get caught.

One time or another, we've all done something "bad" as kids, thinking we'd "gotten away with murder." Briefly share your story. Then invite others to do the same. As always, keep it light at this point in the game.

> What was Achan's sin, and what were the repercussions of his sin?

Achan disobeyed a direct order from God (Joshua 6:17–19, 24). When the Israelites took Jericho, God told them not to take anything; the riches of Jericho were to be put in his treasury. Hoping no one would notice, Achan took a beautiful robe, two hundred silver coins and a wedge of gold (Joshua 7:21). Here is the mind-set that drove Achan's actions: "I saw, I wanted, I took, I hid."

Repercussions: Achan put others in great danger (Joshua 7:2–9); he compromised God's reputation (v. 9); he brought shame and death to his entire family and the nation of Israel (vv. 16–18, 24–26).

There's a lot here . . . keep searching and talking.

What are some of the ramifications of sin we see in the world today?

Think through the news headlines. We see news of greed, corruption, deception, murder, lack of moral judgment, injustice, materialism, etc., in daily publications. We live in a world where it can feel as if anything goes and everyone does just as he wants, ignoring what the outcome will be. And in the end comes death—death of personal sanity, death of civility, death of society, and finally, death of the soul.

How would the story have been different if the guys had told the owner of the house about the gold?

It might have saved their friendship. Obviously, the guy who took the gold would not have died. Maybe the lady would have shared it with the boys. They might have had the opportunity to feel good about themselves for making the right choice. Perhaps it would have really helped the woman. Keep thinking, and you can probably come up with a lot of possibilities.

Describe a time in your life when you went down the wrong road. How did that choice impact your life?

Share an experience from your own life. Remind group members that the guideline of confidentiality is especially important in relation to questions like this one and the next.

What issue(s) of sin are you struggling with in your life right now? What do you fear the ramifications of your sin could be?

Tip: This could be a difficult question. The group may only go as deep as you are willing to go with your answer. Model it first. This could be a breakthrough moment for a person in your group. If you don't feel that the group is willing to jump into such a sensitive topic, have people take time to think about it and do their own silent prayer.

LIQUID would love to thank:

Chris Marcus, for being a producer, designer, editor, and director of photography on the project. You did it all, and we could not have done it without you.

Mariners Church: To the staff and small group department for all of their help and insight into this entire project. And to the congregation and elder board for their prayers and support.

Kenton Beshore, for the beauty of flow questions.

All of the incredible people in North Carolina, who got this whole thing started.

The cast and crew, for the endless hours of hard work and incredible performances.

Aaron and Mark of Tank Creative, for making us sound good.

Cindy Western, for her help in crafting great questions.

Our incredible editor, Kim Hearon, who, to put it simply, had to deal with us. You made it fun.

All the people at Thomas Nelson, for your hard work and expertise.

And we thank God for having his hand on this project and blessing it.